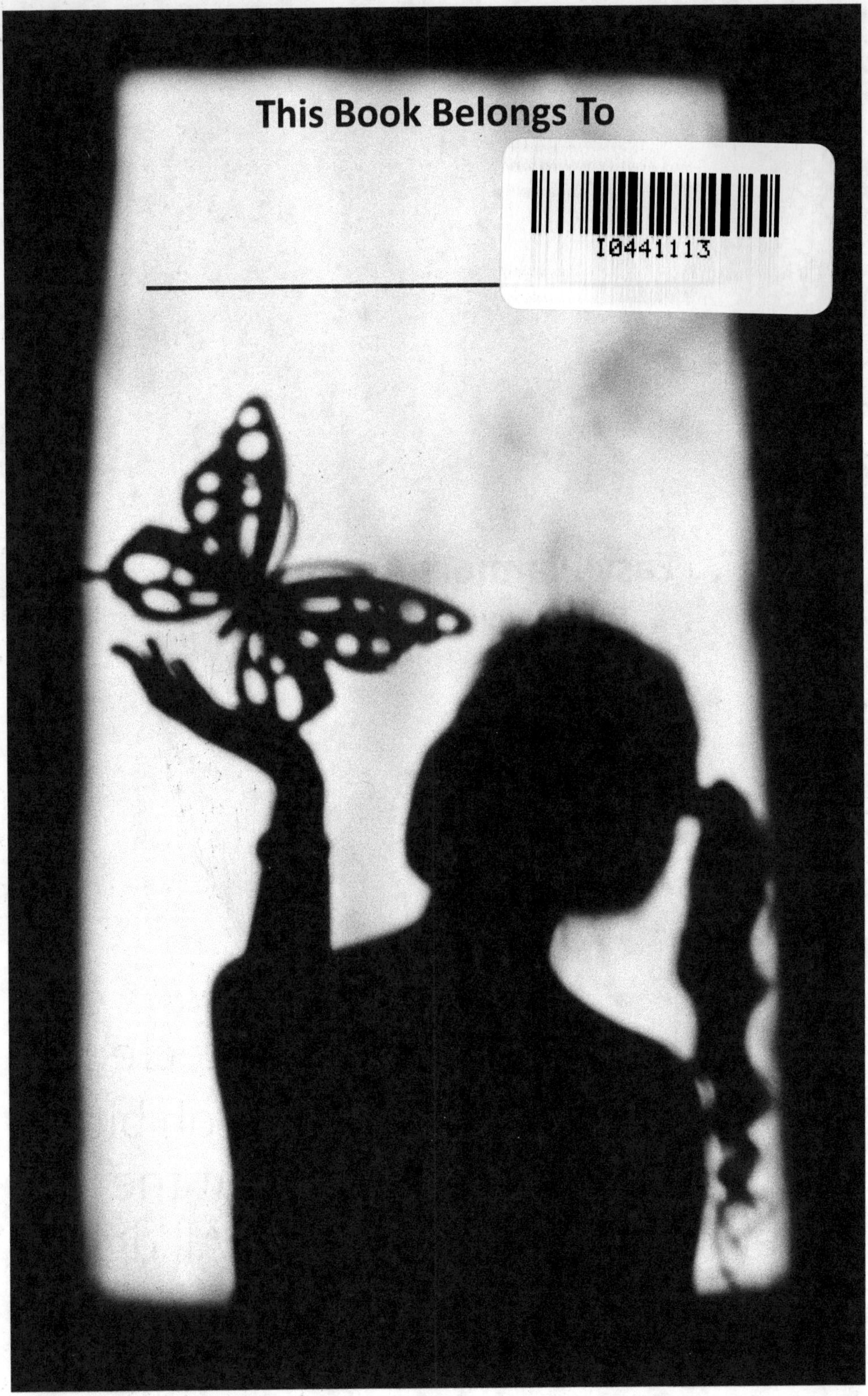
This Book Belongs To

Easy Planners And Journals

To help you organize your life

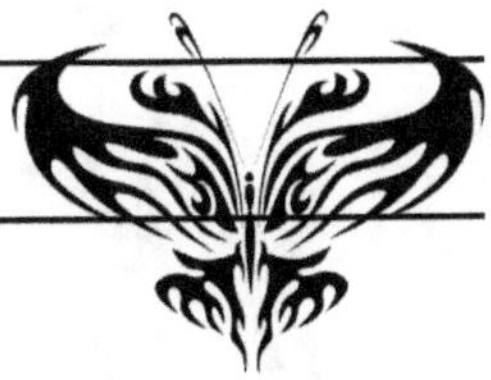

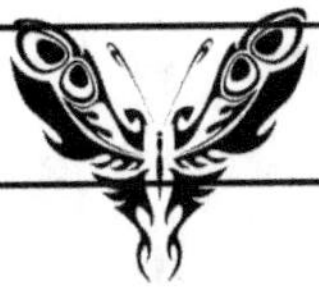

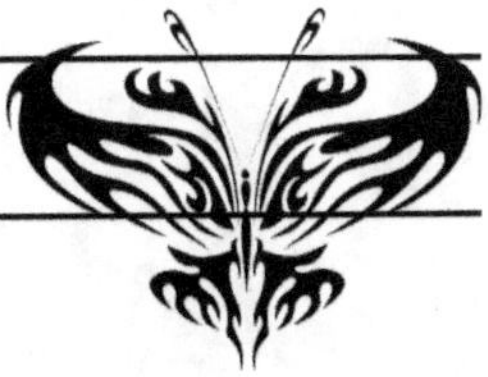

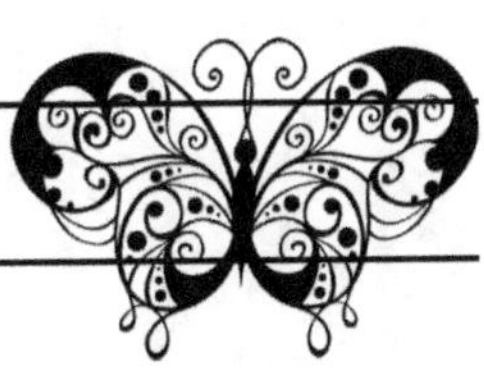

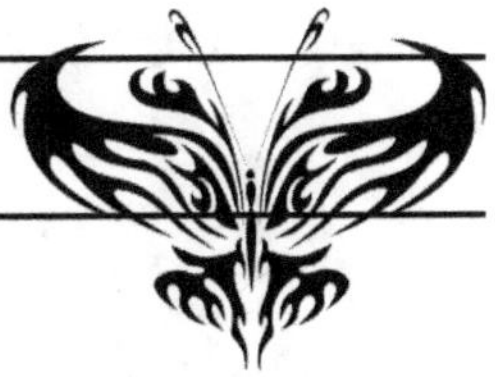

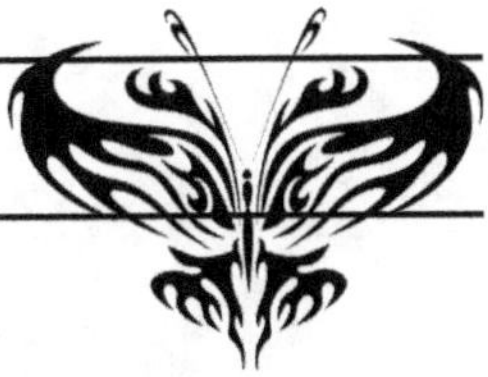

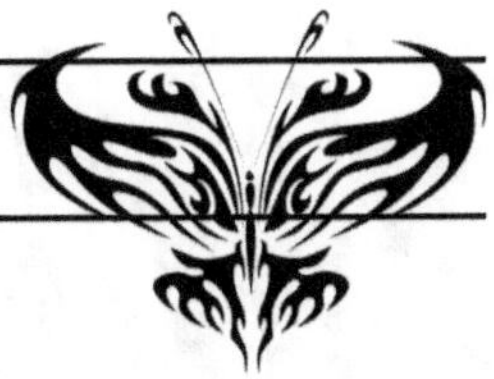

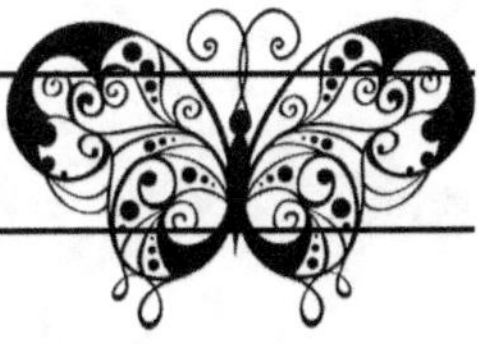

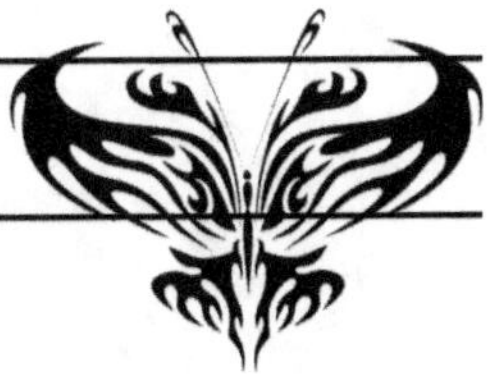

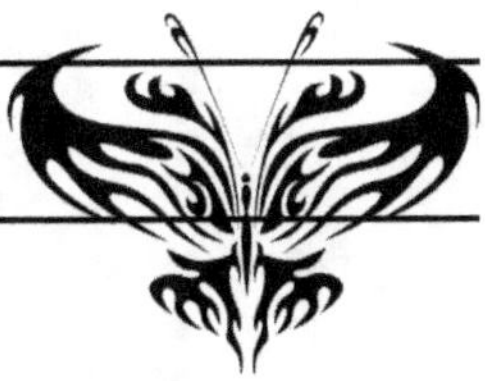

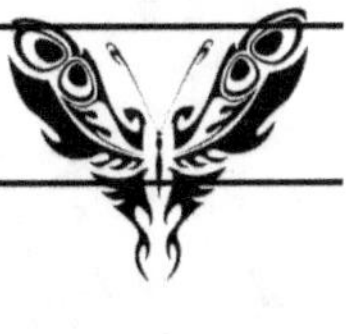

www.ingramcontent.com/pod-product-compliance
Lightning Source LLC
Chambersburg PA
CBHW072050280526
45788CB00006B/2249
9781090552273